Social Di1

Yes You Can!

(Book Two)

How to Grow Your Business

By

Leigh Walton

Social Direct Selling Yes You Can!

Book Two

How to Grow Your Business

By Leigh Walton
First Published in 2014
Copyright by Leigh Walton

The right of Leigh Walton to be identified as the Author of the Work has been asserted by her in accordance with the Copyright, Designs and Patents Act 1988.

Mention of specific companies, organisations, or authorities in this book does not imply endorsement by the author or publisher, nor does mention of specific companies, organisations, or authorities imply that they endorse this book, its author, or the publisher.

All rights reserved.

No part of this publication may be reproduced, or transmitted in any form by any means, electronic or mechanical, including photocopying, recording or any other information storage system, or transmitted, in any form or by any means without the prior written permission of the publisher, nor be otherwise circulated in any form without the written permission of the publisher.

ISBN-13: 978-1503283060
ISBN-10: 1503283062

Why You Should Read This Book!

Book Two builds on the previous book in the series 'Social/Direct Selling – Yes You Can! How to be Successful', and will help you to take your business to a higher level of success.

This guide will teach you how to grow your Social/Direct selling business and how to increase your earning potential. Whether you want to increase the number of product presentations you have booked into your diary, generate higher sales, or build a successful team, this book will arm you with the tools to create a large business which can provide an exceptional income. Leigh has coached and trained Social/Direct sellers to increase their earnings beyond £90,000 ($151,555) per annum.

From learning 'Best Practices', to 'Coaching and Developing People' - Leigh has it all covered for you.

The down to earth and direct advice that Leigh provides (and is known for) is suitable for those fairly new to Social/Direct selling - but willing to push themselves – but also for experienced sellers who want to develop their skills and grow their business!

Pre-Release Reviews

Leigh, this was wonderful! Such fabulous information!
You have given wonderful step by step advice on how to have a successful business in the Direct Sell Industry. Everything you mentioned is so simple and easy to do. This business is fabulous and if we keep it simple we can all be successful!
Sharon Zelen - Independent Executive Director, The Pampered Chef USA

"At last - a truly sensible, comprehensive guide to running a successful direct sales business. Whether you're new to this fast growing business sector, a seasoned pro, or even a corporate trainer, this no-nonsense book will equip you with a simple system, structure and strategy for greater success and rewards. Leigh's years of experience shine through and her concise, easy writing style will ensure that this will become a blueprint for direct sellers to use themselves and for training within their teams."

Marie Burleigh - National Recruitment and Training Manager, Nirvana Spa At Home

"These books are ideal for anyone taking their first steps into the world of Direct Sales, but equally invaluable for long serving Direct Sellers too! They are extremely well written, straight forward and easy to follow. So, in a nutshell, read the book + follow the rules and tips =Social Direct Selling Yes You Can!!"
Jo Egan - Company Director

"Great Read! Tells you all you need to know. It brings back very happy memories of being fortunate enough to work with Leigh - but NOW the next best thing to that, is having this book, it's just like having Leigh beside me!! But for all newbies to the industry - it walks them through it - Step by Step!!"
Lindsay McEwan-Allen – Avon Cosmetics Area Manager

"A fabulously clear, concise, comprehensive guide to succeeding in an industry which is best kept simple. Leigh has written this in a way that can easily be read & implemented by the user, or even as a Training Guide for those delivering training to others"
Vonni Steer – Director citrus7 Ltd (Supplier to DSA)

Dedication

This book is dedicated to the many Social/Direct sellers who have inspired me over the twenty plus years; Daphne Jones who taught me the disciplines of the business and pushed me to over achieve my early goals, Paul Southworth who, without knowing it, set a fine example of never forgetting the names of even the newest recruits.

I want to say a huge thank-you to the friends who proof read and helped edit - Martin Lister especially - and to those who proof read chapters, and encouraged me to carry on - Marie, Joanne, Carolyn, Sarah, Jen and Lynne.

Finally to my family for believing in me as a writer and my husband, Tom, without whose help, support and downright directness (even through my tantrums) this book would never have been finished. He is now my unpaid publisher, senior editor and agent!

Index

Foreword

1. Recruiting

2. Booking Presentations and Host Coaching

3. Building Sales

4. Leading a Team

5. Time Management for Leaders

6. Training and Coaching

7. Coming Out Of Your Comfort Zone.....Often

8. Glossary

9. About Leigh Walton

10. Other Books by Leigh Walton

11. Connect with Leigh Walton

Foreword

In the first book in this series, **'Social/Direct Selling – Yes You Can! How to be Successful'**, you will have learned how to set your business up for success. The topics covered included business skills that you now need to hone for greater success. In addition you will need to teach those skills to your own team members once you start to recruit.

If you have recruited before, the information shared in this second book will help you to sharpen up your recruiting skills, by following simple steps that I have used and taught others to use. One Social/Direct seller found her 'strike-rate' for recruiting greatly improved just because she started to actually 'Close the Sale' by using a simple phrase which I had used for many years before! Others have realised that the use of a potential business plan overcomes many concerns before the prospective recruit voices them! This results in more prospects actually joining your business.

Coaching and Training are covered in detail too. Once you understand the difference between these activities you will become a more effective leader able to train and coach team members to meet their individual needs.

There are many other gems of information in this guide and I hope you not only enjoy reading this book, but put some of the ideas into practise!

If you remember, Book One finished with a chapter on 'Presenting Yourself in Different Situations'. This included presenting yourself at an interview so it seemed natural to begin this book with a chapter dedicated to recruiting!

Chapter 1

Recruiting

Many years ago, successful Direct Selling companies such as 'Tupperware' used to tell their self-employed sales force that '**R**ecruiting **I**s **T**he **A**nswer' - whatever the question! If you want a good income from Social/Direct selling (say £30,000 or $50,000 plus) you need to build a team, thus this old cliché is a good one to bear in mind. This is why you need to be consistently generating recruit leads and looking out for **RITA**!!! This may sound very old fashioned nowadays but guess what? It is still relevant. Of course, **RITA**, could be Matt, Ian, Vince or Tom as well as Emily, Cleo, Gemma, or Leanne.

Men are just as likely to become involved in the Social/Direct selling profession nowadays; back in the 60s and 70s it was mainly women who enjoyed the benefits and successes offered by companies like Avon Cosmetics, Pippa Dee (clothing), and Oriflame (Swedish Skincare). The exception would perhaps have been Tupperware, where couples tended to own and manage their business together.

When I first became an Area Manager with Avon Cosmetics in 1993 I was wary of approaching strangers and there was no way I was going to 'force' any of my family and friends to join as a representative. So, you see, I haven't found this business easy from the start – but it is simple and it is lucrative. It took me around six months to toughen up – coming out of my comfort zone daily by approaching strangers. I have never looked back! I have never had to 'force' anyone to join a Social/Direct selling business – I just had to offer the opportunity, give them all the facts then let them decide.

During my career - winning numerous incentives and achieving the coveted position of being 'Number 1'* Area Sales Manager, (out of around 350 Sales Managers) – whilst working towards an incentive trip to Hong Kong which I achieved - I realised that recruiting really was the answer.

Let me share my **'How To Recruit'** knowledge and experiences with you.

* At the time of publication the listing showing me at No 1 position is in storage. I will endeavour to add this to the book at a later date and will post it on my website.

Recruiting is a process

Remember, you can speed up the process sometimes because you are in control of this, but you will not recruit if you force it. It is the choice of your potential recruit as to whether and when they join your business. I have been very persuasive in the past and on my second visit to those recruits have found they have left a note on the door stating, 'Sorry this is not for me'! Ouch! However, what you can control is the amount of leads you generate in order to recruit plenty of people.

1. What is a lead?

2. How do I qualify a lead?

3. How do I follow up?

4. How long do I follow up for?

Listed above are four good questions to start thinking about. Let's cover the first two questions in some detail.

1. A lead is simply:

Anyone! A living, breathing, human being!

Note: To join a Social/Direct selling company you usually have to be over 18 years of age as the company you are joining will most likely need to credit check or offer credit, to pay for orders placed.

2. 'Qualifying' a lead is fairly easy. The more you do it through effective questioning and developing your listening skills the easier it becomes. Qualifying means finding out if your lead is remotely interested in what you have to offer. If not, then you can always ask for a referral; your lead may 'lead' you to a recruit. Here are some phrases you can try out to help you to qualify leads.

'Do you like (product)?'

'Would you enjoy a little extra money in your pocket every week?'

'Are you a people person?'

'Would you enjoy a paying hobby?'

'Do you absolutely love your current job?'

'Have you ever wanted to be your own boss?'

If you get yes to any of these then you have qualified your lead. You now know that they have a 'need' or a 'want', (hot button) that Social/Direct selling can meet. You need to make a mutually convenient appointment to explain more about the business and the opportunity YOU have to OFFER to THEM. It would be rude not to. I sometimes refer to this as an 'interview' or 'coffee appointment'. However, I wouldn't use 'interview' when offering to meet a prospective recruit. I would be more likely to express that we need to meet up for a coffee and a chat where I can explain a little more about how I can help them to see if (business opportunity) would be a good fit for them.

Can you now see how qualifying a lead is a fairly simple thing to do? You are just finding out a little more information about that person to see whether they have a 'need' or a 'want' that you can help them to meet.

3. You follow up by arranging this meeting within twenty four hours, so that you can give the person enough information on how the business could work for them. It may help to explain that the reason for the meeting is so that they can make an informed choice on whether to join you or not, and so that you can answer any questions they may have. A meeting of around 20-30 minutes is sufficient. Don't be tempted to say you need an hour or two – that is way too much of a time commitment for anyone with the busy lives we all lead today. Conversely, don't be tempted to try explaining about how your business can work for someone in five minutes – it just doesn't work. If you cannot meet in person, arrange a phone call as this is the next best option.

Important!!

Do not ask potential recruits to call you. It won't happen. At least in ninety nine out of one hundred cases it doesn't. You have to call them. After all, it may not be the most pressing event in their diary but generating and following up leads daily **is** the most pressing event in yours! You need to ask, 'When is the best time to call you - daytime or evening?' Arrange to call them and ensure you do so!! If you phrase this as, 'When is the best time to call you?', you may get, 'Oh, anytime', which means you will struggle to catch them. Or, they may say, 'There isn't a good time'. How do you follow up on that? Giving the choice of daytime or evening will avoid any stalling.

4. You follow up until you know that your potential recruit has come to a decision! As a general guide, if you meet or speak to someone, explain all about how your business could work for them and they are undecided, then you need to give them just 24 hours to think on it and discuss it with their family. If you call as arranged, and they are still undecided, then ask them how long they need to come to a decision. If you call again – this is the third opportunity for them to come to a decision – and they are still saying, 'I am not sure I don't think the timing is quite right for me', then I would say, 'OK I don't want to hound you, or waste your time so can I just ask if you are trying to say 'No' to me? If so that is perfectly ok'.

You really don't want to be wasting your time chasing leads which have gone cold or are giving you the run around for whatever reason! Leave the call on a positive – let them know that if they change their mind you will be happy to meet again. This is a dynamic business and you could be out creating new leads rather than following up cold ones.

How to conduct an Interview

When you have your interview (or coffee appointment) booked in the diary, you will feel elated – no matter how many team members you have or how many times you have met up with a prospective new recruit. You may also feel a little nervous if you are new to recruiting, or not experienced, as you will be wondering whether you will leave the meeting with a new team member or not! You need to prepare for this and ensure that, whichever way it goes, you know you have done your best.

In traditional business it is normal for someone to attend at least one interview where we are 'grilled' to see if we are suitable for the position before being offered a job.

But in a Social/Direct selling interview this is reversed. The person you meet for 'coffee' is actually interviewing you! You want your prospective recruit to join your business, so you need to listen carefully to what they are telling you.

Together, with your potential recruit you to need to determine:

1. What the business opportunity can offer them?

2. What are their needs/wants?

3. How the business can fulfil these needs/wants?

4. What the opportunity will do for them by way of personal growth and as a business!

The first thing you need to do is to put your prospective recruit at ease. Don't be tempted to rush into the conversation, telling them what you, or others, achieve, why you joined and what you want out of your business. This interview is all about them...not you!

Here are three simple steps to help you:

1. Do what I call a pre-interview - find out about them

2. Present the business and the company

3. Close the sale

Let's look at these steps in more detail:

Pre-Interview - this should last for around 5 minutes.

No matter how well you think you know your prospective recruit this is your opportunity to find out exactly what their wants/needs (hot buttons) are. Do they want more money, or to build self-confidence. Are they looking to make new friends, or to have a job that is fun? Do they want to be recognised for their achievements, or simply to have me-time instead of being 'someone's mummy/daddy, wife/husband'. Or do they need to have more flexibility in their work life?

Sometimes we are amazed at how little we know even our family members. When we take the time to find out what they want we can be quite surprised! I used to think I knew my family and friends well, until I started asking them more open-ended questions about what they wanted out of life! That old word 'assume' crops up time after time doesn't it?

Encouraging your prospect to tell you about themselves helps them to feel at ease, and assists you when, during the interview, you are aligning the role to their needs/wants. Remember to ask open ended questions as you chat. Open ended questions encourage people to talk, which is exactly what you want in order to find out about them. If you ask closed questions you end up with either a 'Yes' or 'No' answer, which makes it difficult to continue a conversation. An example of a closed question is, 'Do you like to cook?'

Here are some open ended questions to help you to ascertain others needs or wants:

Tell me a little bit about yourself?

What do you enjoy doing?

If you had an extra £50 a week what would you do with it?

What do you do in your spare time?

What would you like to do in your spare time if you had more money?

If you could earn £15-£30 an hour could you reduce hours worked in your usual job - if so would that be beneficial?

Note: With minimum wages being around £6.50 an hour in 2014, this is a good income for many people; of course as you progress and develop a team/larger business this hourly rate increases greatly. For example, your prospective recruit tells you that they work weekends because their company pays them overtime rates, but this means they miss out on seeing their child play sport on a Saturday.

You can then 'sell back their need or want' by explaining:

1. If they could earn their weekend money by joining your business and working five to six hours in the week instead of all day Saturday, this would give them their weekends back.

2. By watching their child play sport they would meet other parents who would be new contacts for their Social/Direct selling business.

This is why it is so important to talk less and listen more during the pre-interview - five minutes of attentive listening tells you a lot about your prospect.

Tip: If you have a shy prospect, help them to come out of their shell by asking open ended questions such as:

What do you enjoy doing?

How long have you lived here?

How many children do you have?

What type of work have you done in the past?

Where do your family live?

Generally, people like to talk. Sometimes you need to gently draw the conversation out of them; a conversation is two-way, otherwise it is a monologue. Don't be tempted to do all of the talking, talk over them, or talk 'for them'.

Introduce the Business Opportunity and the Company

This should last around 20 minutes.

I have described the use of an Opportunity Brochure or Business Presenter in Chapter 8 of Book 1 (How to be Successful). I strongly recommend you use one of these to help you during your presentation of the business opportunity.

This is your chance to present and 'sell' the business opportunity, the company and yourself to your prospective recruit. Never underestimate selling yourself. People buy people. If you are warm and enthusiastic and a good listener, you are half way there!

Prepare for the meeting as best as you can and ensure you have all the information you need to hand. Don't feel you need to memorise the career plan with all of it intricacies – this along with any in-depth information should be listed in your Opportunity Brochure or Business Presenter. Throughout your presentation don't forget to smile, don't rush, don't push, and be truthful. If you don't know the answer to a question tell your prospective recruit that you will find out for them.

You don't always need to go through the Business Presenter/Opportunity Brochure in the order that it is set out. That can come across a little formal and stale. Sometimes it is better to use the pages that will appeal to your prospect first. For example, your brochure may initially refer to information on the background of the company, then the product, then money and incentives to be earned. If your prospect is looking at the role to increase their social circle then information on company background and incentives may not be of the greatest interest. In this situation I would open the brochure at the page that reads 'Where to find Business' whilst explaining that they can launch their business by contacting local clubs and societies, and inviting neighbours to their own 'home presentation'. This demonstrates how Social/Direct selling is a business which will help them to meet people.

During the pre-interview if your prospect voices that they really need an extra £80 a week, then go directly to the page displaying earnings and then take them to 'Where to find business'. You will need to explain that they need to do X number of presentations a week to earn the £80. (See the potential business plan later in this chapter). To achieve the £80 earnings stated above, you would need to carry out 2 presentations - based on a company average of £200 - if the company pays commission of 20%.

Note: You need to have typical figures to use at an interview/coffee meeting. I suggest you take the average customer spend, along with average total sales from a presentation to demonstrate how they make their money!

During this part of the coffee meeting a potential business plan will be the most useful tool you could have to hand. This shows your prospect what the business could do for them.

Take a look at the example below and then I will go on to explain how to use this. If your business operates through presentations, you will find this tool can be copied and used just as it is. If your business operates through the distribution of catalogues, you will need to adapt it accordingly.

	Mon	Tues	Weds	Thurs	Fri	Sat	Sun	Potential Hosts	Potential Guests
Morning								1	1
								2	2
								3	3
								4	4
Afternoon								5	5
								6	6
								7	7
								8	8
Evening								9	9
								10	10
								11	11
								12	12

Number Of Possible Presentations / Week

Earnings From These Presentations

Monthly Earnings Achievable

Other Benefits

How to use the Potential Business Planner

The conversation goes something like this:

You: 'Now that I have told you a little about (business) let's just see if it has the potential to fit into your life and also to give you what are looking for. You told me you would like an extra £80 a week so - Firstly, when would you like to work?'

Prospect: 'Well, I can't do weekdays till after 4pm and I don't really want to do weekends. I go out on a Tuesday evening and my husband goes to the gym on a Thursday evening'.

You: 'Ok, so let's cross those off your planner. Now, you have Monday, Weds and Friday evenings and late afternoons - which is more than enough for two presentations a week, which will give you the income you want. How does that sound and which two slots would you prefer to work?'

Prospect: 'If I said Monday evening and Wednesday evening would that be ok?'

You: 'Sure, I know of someone who does presentations for their ex work colleagues from 6pm till 8pm - this suits as they call in on their way home from work. That way they don't go home and get settled in and then have to go back out!'

Prospect: 'I hadn't thought of that. I assumed all presentations were, say, 8pm onwards! Good idea. OK, I will work Mondays and Wednesdays as that fits in well'.

You: 'Great, that sorts out when you want to work. One of the great benefits of this business is that you are in control of when, where and how you work. Now, let's think about the first twelve people who you could ask to have one of your practise presentations for you. I say practise but you will still earn money of course!'

You then help them to come up with twelve names. These go onto the potential business planner. Any more names given can start going onto their 'List of 100' - this is basically their first contact list.

For these names you will need to prompt your prospect:

Here is a list of questions you can gently ask to begin building their list:

Which neighbours could you ask to host a presentation?

Who is your little boy's best friend? What is his mum called?

Who does your daughter sit by in school? Could you ask her mum or dad to host a presentation?

Which of your friends will most likely host a presentation for you?

Which ex-work or college friends are you still in touch with?

How well do you know your hairdresser? Could you offer them a presentation - at work or at home?

You mention that your husband/wife goes to the gym/tennis club.....who do they know that would help you with a practise presentation?

Which family members are most supportive of you?

The list is endless. I suggest you practise this with family, friends and your 'up-line' so that you can really delve deep and get your prospect off to the most successful start possible.

If you are not going to be selling through group presentations, do the same list for potential customers. I suggest you list at least 30 people if you are going to be selling on a one to one basis. 'Party Planners' have the advantage of one person – the Host - leading them to ten more contacts - the guests at the presentation.

You also need to discuss how your potential recruit will launch their business. A home presentation is a great start. Companies use different terminology for this initial presentation. I believe Product Launch or Business Launch works well and is easily understood. Men in particular are not keen on the word 'party' for a business activity. Once the 'Potential Host' list is completed, you need to help them to list potential guests for their Business Launch. It is a fact that the more guests in attendance, the better the atmosphere. Therefore, the opportunity for potential recruits and future bookings will be increased. In addition to family and friends encourage them to invite neighbours they don't know too well, friends of family members and other acquaintances. This should be the most exciting presentation of all and you need to be there to assist and guide!

Let's now look at the earning opportunity for your prospect. Once you have discussed and agreed how many customers your prospect can practically reach each week you can work out what they may earn. Here are a couple of examples:

Group Presentation

To achieve weekly earnings of £96.00:-

An average presentation with 10 guests would produce £48 earnings.

This is based on 8 guests purchasing at an average spend of £30, giving total sales of £240, at a commission rate of 20%.

One to One selling via the door to door method.

To achieve weekly earnings of £82.50.

Delivering catalogues* to 100 homes over a week would produce £82.50 earnings.

This is based on a ratio of one third of households purchasing at an average spend of £10, giving total sales of £330, at a commission rate of 25%.

* To be cost effective I suggest you order 50 catalogues and distribute these twice.

Note: I have used different guest spend averages and commissions based on my experience in both catalogue delivery and group presentation businesses.

List at the bottom of the potential business plan any other benefits, tangible and non-tangible, that your prospect may receive such as:

Free product incentives on offer in their Start Up period.

Increased self-confidence

Company incentives that could be earned for example a trip away

Having a job that is fun!

Earnings

New friends

Now that you have reached the third stage of the interview you need to ask, 'So how does that sound? It looks like a good fit to me, and you will achieve (mention their needs or wants) too'.

Take a breather here and wait for your prospect to reply. They may well have some questions that you can answer positively for them. Do not dread or evade questions!

Questions mean that someone is interested but not quite 100% sure. It is not your job to convince them to join you. I have done this myself in the past - believe me I have made many mistakes along the way and convincing someone to do something they are not sure about, is one of them! What happens then is that the new recruit either calls to say they have changed their mind, or they don't answer any more calls, which is really frustrating.

It is much better to answer their questions as well as you can, and give them the time they need. If you find you do not know the answer to a question, then jot it down and say you will find out. In practice, this doesn't happen a lot, but find out and get back to them as soon as possible.

Your prospect may have some 'concerns' (these are sometimes referred to as objections in our profession) which you will need to help them to overcome. I will cover common concerns shortly. Concerns can mean that someone is a little unsure as to whether to commit or not; often because they fear failure and think, 'If I join and I can't do the job, or don't get my family and friends support, what then?'

It is your job to help your prospect to overcome their concerns where you can, but if you encounter three concerns in a row then stop and think. What is this person really saying? Are these real concerns, or are they excuses not to join. They may not feel able to actually say 'No' to you face to face; thus you need to draw the truth out, and if it is 'No' you need to accept this – it is not a failure on your part, it is their decision. The reason that people come up with false concerns is that they feel you are in the stronger position in this situation. They may have warmed to you and feel they have wasted your time, so, rather than say a direct 'No', they try to come up with reasons as to why they can't join. Strange but true!!

Common Concerns

Can I do this?

Will I be successful?

What if I fail?

Will I really make any money?

Do I know enough people to find enough customers?

What are the ongoing costs?

How do I raise the money for the starter kit?

What notice do I need to give if I want to leave?

Will my family support me?

Is it a proper job?

What will my professional colleagues think of me?

I am not a salesperson!

Do any of these sound familiar? I bet they do!

People voice these concerns by saying:

I don't think I have the time

My partner wouldn't like me doing this

I don't have enough friends

My friends don't have any money to buy the product

I can't afford the starter kit

I don't have the confidence to speak to a group of people

I can't do what you do

My family won't support me

Overcoming Concerns

If you have used the potential business planner then you will have already overcome the following concerns:

I don't think I have the time (they have already told you when they could work).

I don't have enough friends (with your help they have identified 12 potential Hosts or 30 potential Customers).

As for, 'My friends don't have any money to buy the product', I always say, 'Actually, if they come to the presentation they don't have to spend. They can touch and feel the products and then it's their choice as to whether, and how much, they spend. Also, remember that if they book their own presentation from yours they will end up saving money, because hosts receive free and/or discounted product as a thank-you'.

To help overcome lack of confidence, or family not being supportive, explain that this is a completely normal reaction.

Offering to do their first presentation with them will help to build confidence. You could also give them the chance to accompany you to one of your presentations where they get to help you to present the product.

When people tell me that they do not have a supportive family I explain that this is quite common! Sometimes family are just being over-protective and come across as being non-supportive. Sometimes it is because they are simply 'dream snatchers' and don't want to see others being successful.

If cash for the starter kit is a concern, ask if a credit card be used for the purchase? As long as the new recruit works their first four shows and then pays off the credit card with monies earned (before interest becomes due) this may be a solution.

Note: I do not encourage the use of credit cards unless you can pay them off in full each month!

One concern that you may think you can't overcome at this stage is, 'I need to ask my partner'. To help I have a top tip for you which an ex-colleague shared with me a while back:

As you take your prospect through the potential business plan ask, 'If you were to join a business like this would it be your own decision or someone else's?' If they reply, 'My own decision', jot this down anywhere on the potential business plan. You then know that you really are speaking directly to the decision maker!

Closing the Sale

This is a common term for ending the interview and asking your prospect if they are going to join your business. Sounds a little scary? Maybe, but if you don't ask directly you won't know how your prospect is feeling. You need to know what their thoughts are, whether they want to get started right away or whether they need time to think about things.

I know of many experienced Social/Direct sellers who just do not close the sale. They are left:

Wondering **when** to follow up

Wondering **if** to follow up

Wondering **how** to follow up

This is not a good feeling, believe me. Your prospect thinks, 'Oh well, perhaps they don't think I am capable of working the business', or, 'Perhaps they don't want me on their team'. You think, 'What did I do wrong there", and, 'Should I wait for them to call me?'

In actual fact 'closing the sale' is simple. Once you have done your presentation, and overcome any concerns, just relax, smile, sit back a little - to give some space between you and your prospect - and say, 'So Jade, would you like to join my team?'

Then wait for their reply and act accordingly.

If they come up with a concern that you have covered, such as, 'I need to chat to my partner', say, 'Ok, I understand, although you said it would be your own decision to join the business earlier on. Is this still the case....?' They may simply reply, 'Yes, but out of courtesy I want to talk it through'. That's absolutely normal and OK.

Whilst voicing that this is OK you could also explain that to enable the starter kit to be despatched quickly, it would be easier to complete the paper work whilst you are together Then, when you call them to confirm their decision (remember this needs to be within 24 hours maximum) there is no further hold up. This may sound a little assertive but this is your business and you have invested your time in this person. If you have to meet again then your hourly rate is diluted. If they are serious they will see the sense in this and it will be a good lesson for them once they start to recruit. Time is money!

Another simple phrase that I know to be successful when closing the sale is to simply voice, 'I would love to have you on my team Jo. Shall we get the paperwork done?'

If you have done your job well, by meeting their needs and wants, why would your prospect not at least, 'Give it a go'? Nobody is signing up for life. The agreements issued by bona fide Social/Direct selling companies give rights to the newly recruited person to cancel their starter pack within a certain period (30 days is usual). In addition to this when people decide to leave the business, at any point in their career, they don't have to give notice. Social/Direct selling is an 'easy to join, easy to leave', very low risk business. Sometimes people are just too sceptical to believe it!

Once you have 'closed the sale', if your prospect has decided to join, you can begin their training right away – time allowing! Hand them a blank monthly planner (you can find these on various websites) and ask them to pencil in the dates of upcoming company trainings, team meetings, potential presentations or one to one appointments, and their own Business Launch date. Book them into your (or your up-lines) next 'New Recruit Training' session and welcome them warmly to your team. This is the start of a new business relationship; you owe it to them to get them off to the most successful start.

If your prospect has decided not to join then firstly find out if this is, 'No, not now', or 'No, never'.

If 'not now' ask when they would like you to contact them next.

If it is, 'no. never', then thank them for talking to you.

Ask who they know that may be interested in knowing more about your business. Also ask if they would book a product presentation with you. Referrals* are always welcome!

Don't ever be tempted to leave 'in a grump' because you feel they have wasted your time, you never know who they may refer on to you.

* A referral is simply a name (address, email and telephone number) of another person who you can contact to offer one of your opportunities to. That could be the offer to see a catalogue, to host a product presentation or to look at the business opportunity!

As you may have read in Book 1 of this series, customers and hosts often become team members when they realise the potential earnings - and other benefits - that a Social/Direct selling business can bring. Using the information shared in this chapter, and Chapters 4 and 6 of this book, here is a diagram depicting what could happen as long as you inform and invite every single customer and host to find out more about how your business could work for them:

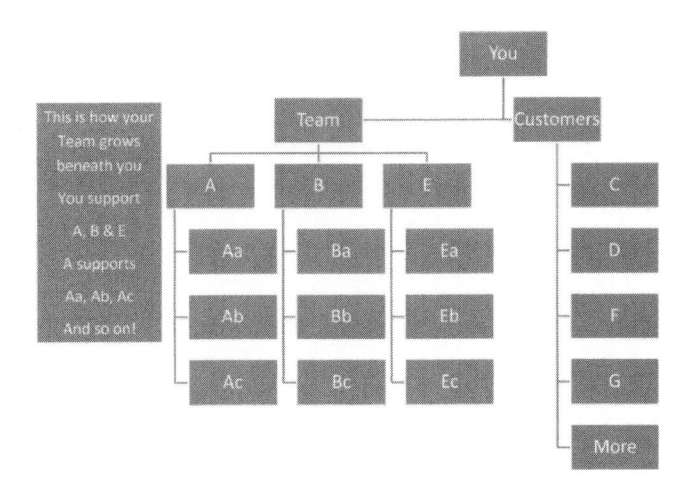

```
                                    You
                                   /    \
This is how your        Team              Customers
Team grows            / | \                  |
beneath you          A  B  E                 C
You support          |  |  |                 D
A, B & E             Aa Ba Ea                F
A supports           Ab Bb Eb                G
Aa, Ab, Ac           Ac Bc Ec              More
And so on!
```

Now onto the bigger picture: Once you become skilled at generating and qualifying leads, converting the majority of your leads, and then training, coaching, motivating and inspiring your team to duplicate what you do, the diagram below is what your team could look like within a year. Social/Direct selling is a numbers game (you will have heard this many times by now) and a simple business. It is based on recruiting, taking bookings for product presentations and selling product yourself. Once you get those three steps in the correct order by looking for recruits first, then bookings, then sales, your business and your earnings will grow exponentially.

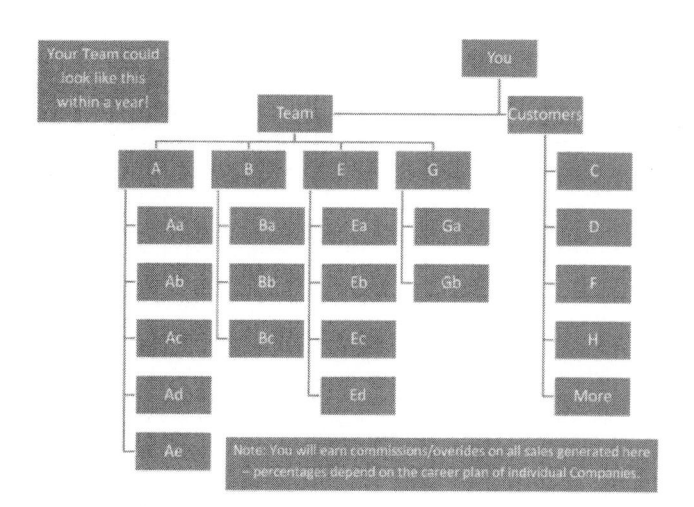

Your Team could look like this within a year!

- You
  - Team
    - A
      - Aa
      - Ab
      - Ac
      - Ad
      - Ae
    - B
      - Ba
      - Bb
      - Bc
    - E
      - Ea
      - Eb
      - Ec
      - Ed
    - G
      - Ga
      - Gb
  - Customers
    - C
    - D
    - F
    - H
    - More

Note: You will earn commissions/overrides on all sales generated here – percentages depend on the career plan of individual Companies.

Chapter 2

Booking Presentations

Presentations are the life blood of your business; without them you don't have a business. When you first join a Social/Direct selling company you won't have any presentations booked into your diary, which is why you need to build a list of contacts. This 'warm' list will be what you work on to launch your business. As you begin to contact these people, and offer them the opportunity to book you for a presentation, you need to carry on adding new names and building the list. In Social/Direct sales your contact list is sometimes referred to as a 'List of 100'. If you aim for 100 names from different areas of your life such as colleagues from where you work or have worked, old school and college friends, neighbours, acquaintances from clubs where you are a member, family, extended family, church, parents you come into contact with through your children etc., you will easily go beyond this number and your business will benefit from it.

During the first couple of days of your new business, you should have had a meeting with your recruiter (up-line) in order to work together on expanding this list. At the very least you need a minimum of twelve potentials hosts, or thirty potential customers, depending on how you are going to work. If you are struggling to build your list of 100 make sure you ask for help. Your recruiter or their team leader will have many ideas of groups of people that you may not think of straight away.

The ideal situation at any point in your career is to have the next six weeks filled with firm bookings. Why? Because, we book our next round of presentations from these! For example, if you do a presentation on Wednesday 26 February, and your next five/six weeks are fully booked, you will be looking to fill week commencing Monday 7 April. This gives the new Host enough time to plan for their presentation. Most people need a little time to think about who they will invite, plus they will want to make sure the house is tidy and the rest of the family are occupied on the date of their presentation!

Of course, it doesn't always work so smoothly. You may find yourself with a date which you need to fill in the next week or so. I refer to these as 'Close-In Bookings'. In this case you would offer this date to the first guest to book their own presentation. Consider offering a small incentive to encourage them to do so.

Alternatively, you may find someone wants to book a presentation but is selling their home and wants to book you for when they are settled in their new home, which could be six months away. I refer to these as Long Dated Bookings.

Both of these situations will crop up but the ideal is to be booking around six weeks in advance.

At each group presentation you need to be aiming to book two more. Why? If you remember, in Chapter 7 of Book 1 (How to be Successful), you completed a Time Studies exercise where I referred to 'Growing' your business as opposed to 'Managing' your business. If you want to 'Grow' you need to do more than 'replace' the presentation you are currently doing.

Look at it like this. Every presentation needs at least one booking to replace it. Otherwise, after your first six or so presentations, you will have run out of business.

If you just book the 'replacement presentation' and then that person has to cancel, your business will be going backwards. If you aim to book two, and one person cancels, then at least your still have a 'replacement presentation'. However, if both presentations take place then you are building your bookings, growing your business, increasing your sales and earning more money! The very nature of life is that people can fall ill, or something crops up so that they have to postpone or even cancel presentations that they booked with you in good faith. I want to stress this point because I have known Social/Direct sellers to say, 'I just wouldn't have time to do more than one presentation a week so I only ever look for one new booking'.

Let me tell you a secret....if you did start generating more bookings than you could handle you would either realise what a lucrative business you have and decide to make it your career, or you could pass excess bookings to any team members you have or even to your up-line who would be able to allocate them to someone else in the team. When this happens others usually reciprocate.

Most people who don't generate bookings from presentations are not taking the time to 'create the want', for each guest. Answering honestly, do you begin your presentation knowing something about each guest? Do you know what would appeal to them about hosting a presentation? Or do you focus only on the Host when doing your host coaching and setting up for the presentation? I will cover how you can 'create the want' with virtually every single guest towards the end of this chapter.

At each group presentation you need to ask every single person if they would like to enjoy some free/discounted product by simply hosting their own group presentation.

Note: How would you feel if someone offered every person in the room a chocolate but missed you out? This is how guests that you haven't offered the opportunity to host their own presentation will feel.

Now that you are thinking, 'OK maybe I do need to go all out for two bookings' I am going to challenge you to stretch for three!!!

Why?

Because it is just as simple and more lucrative; if you are serious about your business you will know that the more bookings you have, the more solid your business.

The third booking will often come from your host. Every single host needs to be given the opportunity to receive free/discounted product at least twice a year. Their guests will be only too happy to attend again if they have enjoyed the presentation. In most Social/Direct selling companies you will have new product to launch at least twice a year, so don't assume the guests will not want to see you and your 'shop' again.

Create a habit of saying to your host as you are confirming their choice of thank-you gift, 'What I usually do is re-book my host in around six months' time when your friends will most likely want to see the new products that will be available. Shall I pencil you in for (suggest a date) and we can confirm nearer the time?'

If a host declines what have you lost? If half of them are happy to re-book, but then cancel at a later date, what have you lost?

Imagine if you presented just one group presentation a week (fifty two a year), and re-booked fifty percent of those (twenty six), yet half of those then cancelled, that would still provide you with thirteen extra presentations a year.

At an average presentation of £300 that £3,900.00 incremental sales!

Tip: On your way to every presentation repeat to yourself, 'I'm never through till I've booked two!' –and that does not include offering your host a long-dated booking!

How to Generate Bookings

During your presentations you need to voice plenty of (what are known in the industry as) 'Booking Bids'. A mix of subliminal and direct booking bids work well.

Here are a few subliminal bids which you could try out:

1. 'When you host your own presentation you get X amount of product free/discounted'.

2. 'If you can't quite stretch to purchasing all of the products you want this evening, I would be happy to come and do a presentation for you, to enable you to receive some free product'.

3. 'I do daytime and evening presentations, so let me know which would suit you best'.

4. 'My last host ended up with £xx of product free!'

Direct booking bids need to be used when you are taking orders, or have one to one contact with guests; try these:

1. 'Sam, I would be delighted to come to your home and do a presentation for you and your friends. Which products would you like to receive free of charge or discounted?'

2. 'You may remember that I mentioned my last host received £xx of product free –how does that sound to you? Would you enjoy receiving some free product?'

3. 'Was there anything you loved today that you would like at a discount, or free of charge?'

4. 'I am taking bookings now for (month), would you like to book a date with me, or would another month suit you better?'

Tip: Before, during, and after your presentation, use both ears to listen to what the guests are saying. With time, you can really hone this skill; when you know who is saying that they love the product, but are short of money or think it is a little expensive, you can tactfully offer them their own presentation when you discuss their order or say good-bye to them.

Booking presentations, just like recruiting, is all about selling back a need or want!

In addition to verbal booking bids, you need to use visual booking aids. It is a fact that people learn and respond to their environments differently. We have five senses; the more of these you cover, the more likely you are to reach everyone.

If you are selling a food product you should aim to cover all senses within your presentation. This is why so many food businesses succeed. Even the aroma of bread baking or fresh coffee can cause us to stop in our tracks:

1. Sight

2. Hearing

3. Touch

4. Taste

5. Smell

With any other product you should at least aim to cover three senses, those of:

1. Hearing

2. Sight

3. Touch

Note: Don't ignore the fact that one or more of the people you are addressing may suffer from a lack of one or some of these senses.

Not everyone will be avidly listening to you throughout the presentation so let's think about visual booking aids that you can use to evoke interest in what you have to offer.

Firstly, have one or two pictorial monthly calendars printed off with your chosen work slots highlighted. As you pass these around, or refer to them, inform your guests that you are lucky enough to work when you choose - which is just one of the benefits of your job that you enjoy. This doubles up as a recruiting bid too. Explain that the highlighted slots are free and if they pop their name and telephone number down you will reserve that slot for their own presentation.

Tip: To encourage bookings you could say, 'If the slot is highlighted in red that means you get an additional gift for booking'.

This is a good way of ensuring you gain bookings when you want or need them. The additional gift could be a bottle of inexpensive sparkling wine, a box of chocolates, six homemade cup-cakes etc. We all like something for nothing! Alternatively a relevant booking gift would be a magazine relative to the product you are presenting. If your product is food related try a copy of Delicious magazine, if you are presenting jewellery or clothing try a magazine such as 'Glamour'.

Cleanly written, informative posters work well as a visual aid too. Purchase a couple of plastic stands to advertise both the business opportunity and bookings. If the company you are associated with supply these, then use those. If not make some smart posters on a computer – hand written posters are a no-go. Ensure that visual aids like this are in large dark font so that they can be read easily from a distance. On your Bookings poster list the benefits of holding a presentation; if you have monthly booking incentives make sure they are clearly explained.

Whilst guests are chatting to each other, listening to the presentation, or simply sipping a drink they need to be able to see these visuals easily so place them on window sills, over the fireplace, and on the table showcasing your products.

Now for a slightly 'off-the-wall' idea

Using several pages of A4 paper, list the generic benefits that hosts can enjoy; one per page with pictorial evidence to back them up works well. Laminate and tape these pages together then add a couple of blank sheets to the top of the list so that your first benefit is not hidden from view. Next, fold the sheet alternately so that as you open them up they concertina out as you hang the list over a door, or on something like a curtain rail/mirror/painting on the wall.

I have listed some generic benefits for you to get the idea.

Fun

Free Product

Discounted Product

Chance to shop from you seat - not your feet

Spend time with friends

Get to know neighbours

Try before you buy

Special host offers

Chance to raise funds for a charity/group of your choice

Note: I know of someone who did just this and hung it over the bathroom door so that when guests visited the bathroom they could take a couple of minutes to peruse host benefits!

Creating 'The Want'

Remember that your host is a valuable resource who will know their guests better than you do. During host coaching, when you chat about guests, ask them who has confirmed attendance and say, 'Tell me a little about (Jim) so that I can make sure I bring along something that will appeal to him'.

Whilst setting up your product display, engage your host in conversation about their guests. Explain that you need to know a little about each guest so that you can tailor parts of the presentation to the guests -this is common sense to me.

After all, if you are selling cosmetics to a group of thirty something's you will not want to focus them on products for teenage or mature skin, however, they may want to buy gifts for someone in those age ranges so it stills pays to mention them. Similarly, if you are selling cookware to a group of people aged fifty plus you probably won't want to harp on about cooking fish fingers and chips! When you know a little about each guest, you will be able to throw in comments that speak to them on an individual basis. It takes practice to hone this skill – a good memory helps. You will find your memory starting to retain necessary information like this more and more, as you practise. That is one of the benefits of Social/Direct selling that surprised me!

In the early days, I suggest you focus on just two or three of the guests that, in your opinion, (see list below) are most likely to book you for their own presentation. Don't forget that you still need to offer EVERYONE a presentation of their own when you take their order!

Most likely to book are:

Social butterflies – the people who love holding and going to parties

Those who enthuse about your product

Guests who bring a friend along

Guests who were a little apprehensive about coming

Anyone who has hosted in the past for another consultant who had now left the company

Anyone who has recently moved house, or had renovations done; as they may want to 'show off' their house

Taking the above into account, chat conversationally to the host as you are setting up, and try to identify your 'most likely to book' guests. You can take this one step further by chatting to guests as they arrive. Use name badges so that as you welcome them and write out their name, you can say something like, 'Hi Beth, Martin mentioned that you have recently moved house – have you settled in to your new place?'

Or:

'Nice to meet you Max, George said you love cooking. What type of recipes do you prefer to cook?'

Build on this rapport throughout the presentation by making eye contact and smiling at your guests. When discussing or taking orders, refer back to what you now know is their 'hot button'. For Max this may be learning a new recipe. For Suzi, it could be acquainting herself with her new neighbours.

The skill of being able to build rapport with people you have just met takes time to perfect; however, the more you practise, the more skilled you become.

To recap, you need to offer everyone the opportunity to host a presentation. You need to use plenty of indirect and direct verbal booking bids. In addition you need to use visual booking aids as mentioned earlier in this chapter like the concertina sheets and the posters. Other visual aids could be a well-placed stack of catalogues, several opportunity brochures scattered around the room, labels placed on product which read 'I am part of the starter kit – ask your demonstrator for details' and so on. Your products are the most prominent visual aid you have – keep them in good condition.

Note: There is a possibility of booking presentations with blind, deaf and otherwise disabled people. Just because they have a disablement doesn't mean they don't shop! Why should they be ignored? I was contacted many years ago by an organiser who wanted an interesting and fun evening for a group of deaf people. They provided a signer for me, and after a successful night one of the guests joined my team where she built a profitable and enjoyable business. To enable her to partake in telephone training we used a medium called 'Type-Talk'. There are many more sophisticated forms of communication available nowadays to aid disabled people. This is simply food for thought - and is a relatively untapped market!

Host Coaching (for group presentations)

Host coaching is sometimes perceived as an activity that is not critical. I have heard many Social/Direct sellers say, 'It's OK if I've got the time to do it'. However, I believe it is one of the most beneficial and imperative activities. It will:

1. Increase your earnings

2. Bring you future business

3. Ensure your host is most likely to re-book you

4. Bring you great P.R. When your hosts tell their friends how easy hosting was, they are sure to want to book you too

Host coaching is best done in the following 3 steps:

1. The first step begins when a person agrees to host for you. As soon as they book their presentation you need to give them a pack of information relevant to hosting. (Check with the company you have joined for a finite list of contents.) I suggest the pack includes a couple of catalogues and order forms for those guests who can't attend, information on your 'Host Reward System', and brief information on the business opportunity (so that they can read and digest before the presentation – if they like what they see they may join you). Next, agree a date and time to do the in-depth host coaching call or visit (see stage 2 below). Be sure to explain that you will need around twenty minutes for this, which is why you prefer to book firmly into both yours and their diaries. You also need to let hosts know that if they wish to postpone for any reason you need notice so that you can re-book their slot (otherwise you will suffer loss of earnings just like any job). How much notice is up to you but I would ask for a week.

2. The second stage usually takes place by way of a phone call or face to face visit about two weeks before the presentation. This is when you need to explain exactly how the presentation will flow and how they can help. People who host a presentation want it to be a successful event as it reflects on them– nobody likes egg on their face! The purpose of host coaching is to guide and support so that your host has fun, earns free product and enjoys the presentation. When you host coach effectively the result should be a good number of guests in attendance who are interested in what you have to show them. This makes your job easier, fun and lucrative. When at this stage of host coaching I suggest you say something like, 'Jackie, I will do my very best to ensure that you have a fun presentation, and receive plenty of free products as a thank you; we will be working as a partnership throughout your presentation, does that sound OK? Great, let me explain how the presentation works and what help I need from you'. Then discuss:

a. How you would like the room set up for the presentation.

b. Check if there is a table available to display your products. If not then I suggest you purchase an inexpensive, lightweight, folding table, or find out if you can make use of a breakfast bar/chest of draws or similar.

c. Whether you want guests seated or standing/milling around.

d. The format of the presentation – running order, and whether it is formal, informal, or a mix.

e. How long you require to set-up your product prior to arrivals.

f. How long the evening will last and what time you anticipate finishing.

g. The host will want to provide light refreshments but keep it simple; soft drinks before, perhaps nibbles and choice of drinks after. Advise your host not to serve drinks or nibbles during the presentation or else you will lose the guests attention! Remember - an informed and organised host is a happy host. When you run through how the presentation works do take a breather and check occasionally, 'Does that sound OK to you?' Host coaching is a dialogue, not a monologue. In addition, find out if your host understands the host thank-you/reward scheme. Take them through this thoroughly (use different intonation in your voice to express your enthusiasm - enthusiasm is infectious and you want them to be enthusiastic too). Encourage them to want to achieve all benefits on offer. Usually, the higher the sales the more rewards on offer. It is worth rewarding your host for bookings generated from their presentation too (your company may already do this).

3. The final stage of host coaching takes place a day or so before the presentation. Make a quick call to let your host know you are excited about their presentation and looking forward to seeing them and their friends. Check that you know exactly where you are going and find out if you can park close (essential if you have a heavy product to transport). Check how many guests are coming and suggest ways to build the guest list if it is low in numbers. This call can turn a 'possibly panicking' host, just about to postpone or cancel into a, 'calm, keep the date' host. How? Well, imagine a host has had four or five people who suddenly call to say, 'Sorry I can't make the date after all'. They are bound to feel like they are wasting your time and will look like Billy-no-mates on the day. However, if you run through the guest list with them you can suggest that each guest brings along someone like a work colleague, a relative, a friend, a neighbour. You can help them to double the number of guests at this last stage with some suggestions and creative thinking, and rescue the presentation!

When you implement these 3 steps, you will find that your host gets more out of her presentation, you get more sales and bookings out of it, and your business moves to a higher level of success.

Note: A word of common sense. If someone books with you today for a presentation in five days' time combine steps 2 and 3. If they book with you today for a date in six months' time then you may want to add in a 'touch-base' call or two, just to keep the contact going!!!

Fact: I have heard of instances of Social/Direct sellers arriving at a house to do a presentation and finding the house in darkness. Usually the host had not been coached and had possibly forgotten that they had booked a presentation. Or maybe they simply thought, 'Well the person from (company) can't be coming as I haven't heard a word since I booked with them!'

Chapter 3

Building Sales

I have been told many times over the years, by successful Social/Direct sellers that:-

'The products sell themselves'.

That may be the case; however, if it were, surely it would leave us without a purpose? Why would we need to attend a presentation? Why wouldn't we just drop a variety of products off to a host then pop back to collect orders later on?

There are several reasons. One is that we want to interact with our customers as we are more likely to gather repeat and additional sales from them once we have done so. In addition we are more likely to acquire future bookings, recruit leads and referrals when we are face to face with customers. Another reason is that we can build sales and increase our earnings through presenting our product well.

Let's look at several simple ways to build sales.

Display

Your product display is your shop window. What you display and how you display it will impact on your sales. You don't need to be a professional window dresser in order to arrange your products well but here are a few pointers which will help:

1. The products need to be clean and in good working order. If you are displaying cosmetics that are to be used as samples, make sure you clean the containers every time you put them away. Check that your lotions and potions have enough products left in them. Customers are not impressed if they pick up an almost empty container and have to literally try and scrape out the remaining product in them. If you are displaying clothing check that your samples are clean and pressed. It helps if you pack them away in plastic bags or tissue paper to prevent creasing. Who wants to try on a shirt that looks as though it has been worn?

2. Theme your display! For instance, leading up to Easter use some small chocolate eggs and a fresh bunch of daffodils to brighten up your table. If Mother's or Father's Day is imminent display some nice gift ideas in clear cellophane and tied with ribbon. During autumn, accessorise your display with deep reds, green, brown and aubergine -use fruit and vegetables if your product is cookware or health-food. To add interest to clothes, dress up your display with inexpensive scarves or jewellery. If you sell books, use a smart cloth to dress your display table and vary the display. Have some books open, use small boxes covered in appropriate wrapping to give the display some height. Books for children look inviting on cloth or paper in primary colours, or you may find material with the alphabet on. Fun book ends add instant appeal! Magazine or newspaper articles relevant to your product, or relevant to the idea of Social/Direct selling as a business, are a great addition to a display. They may sow seeds in the minds of potential customer and recruits. Display these articles in clear flexi-frames to enable people to pick them up and read them.

3. If you are attending an event or show make sure you know the audience. You may not have room to display every single product from your range. Think about which products will be most appealing. If you were selling nutrients and had a stand at a local gym you may want to draw attention to the body-building products. If you were at a slimming club you may want more focus on the weight loss products.

4. Have company literature arranged neatly at the side of your product display so that you have information to hand should you need to find a price, or information on a product, quickly.

5. Don't use handwritten notes to grab attention. They don't! Well they do - but not in a good way. I once saw a well organised display ruined by handwritten coloured cardboard stars with prices and special offers.

6. Group products in odd numbers; three or five work well. You can have three products which work well together or three of one product.

Link Selling

Link selling, or layering as it is sometimes known in the cosmetic industry, is just what it 'says on the tin'. You will have several products in your range which are designed to complement each other. It is important for you to get to know your products to enable you to link-sell with confidence. Take some time now to jot down half a dozen products from your product range – these can be your best sellers or just six products that you love. Next to each of these, write down as many other products from your range that would make an ideal addition to each product.

Let me share a couple of examples:

1. A kitchen-ware company sells beautiful stainless saucepans. If I were selling these I would automatically explain to my customer that to keep them looking their best I recommend they use a silicone coated whisk for making sauces in the pan as a metal whisk may scratch. In addition I could link-sell wooden spoons (as opposed to metal for the same reason) and micro-fibre cloths for washing up as they won't scratch like a scouring pad would.

2. A beauty company sells some excellent Spa products. Customers purchasing their body scrub ought to be offered the chance to buy the body wash and body cream too (in the same fragrance) as the wash will not only help rinse off the scrub but will enhance the fragrance. The cream will seal the fragrance in and keep the skin soft. Finally, the fragrance will last much longer if the products are used together in a layering effect.

Note: Link-selling isn't pushing or forcing customers to buy, but will make a big difference to your sales. Looking at it from the customer's point of view, imagine if you purchased the afore-mentioned saucepan and (without advice from the salesperson) used a metal whisk and scratched the pan. How annoyed would you be if you hadn't been made aware of the benefit of a silicone whisk?

My philosophy is that the person selling me a product or a service usually knows more about what they are selling than I do – therefore I am happy to listen to their advice. I can then make an informed decision as to whether to purchase their recommendations, or not!

Add-Ons

Add-ons are items of low cost that would make a useful little purchase for almost anybody. Most people have 'present drawers' nowadays, for those last minute occasions when they need a little gift for a thank-you gift or an inexpensive birthday present for around £5-10.

Which of your products retail in this price bracket? Make a list of them now. You may have jotted down; a cookbook at £5, a pair of earrings costing £10, a hand-cream for £6 - all of these make for add-ons. Why not mention these after your presentation? You could simply say, 'I have a super hand cream for only £6, you may want to add one to your order for your present drawer'.

Note: Some Social/Direct selling companies have 'spend and receive' offers whereby customers spending £XX receive a free product. When you have a customer who has placed an order, but not quite reached the spend level needed, it is only courteous to remind them of this and offer an 'add-on' or 'buy-the-way' product. Just say, 'Thanks for your order – by the way, if you added the hand cream I mentioned earlier on for just £6 do you realise you will get (spend and receive product) free?

As always, let them make the decision.

In case you think you've picked up a misspelling I have previously mentioned 'buy the way' in Chapter 8 of Book 1 (How to Be Successful)!

Promotions

If you were a fully independent business owner you would, no doubt, look to put on seasonal promotions and sales. As a Social/Direct selling business trader you will need to work within guidelines set by the company you have joined.

I have known of people in our profession that offer their own sales and incentives such as, 'Spend £X and get 10 percent discount' or 'Buy two and get one free'. However, consider this scenario:

You have a new team member who has joined because they have a real need to earn money from day one and recoup their investment. They cannot afford to give any discount as this comes out of their commission. Is it really fair, or sensible, for you or other established team members to put these offers on?

I have first-hand experience of newer team members telling me that they have been at the order taking stage of a presentation when a guest has said, 'I purchased something off Jo Blogs last week who gave me a 10 percent discount. Unless you can do the same I won't consider purchasing tonight'. Ouch! I really want to re-iterate the point that these offers do cause newer consultants to strongly consider leaving. This does not sit well with hosts either because the reduced sales caused by the discounting mean less benefits for the host.

However, do be aware of all promotions, incentives and sales that your chosen company do offer to increase sales. Ensure you fully understand and promote these.

Finally, if you do want to offer your own promotion as a one off to boost sales, never be tempted to do so when a company promotion is running. Promotions on top of promotions are referred to as piggy-backing – there really is no need for it!

Chapter 4

Leading a Team

When you recruit your first team member you will start to enjoy additional benefits!

Whether the benefit comes in the form of a reward from the company for recruiting, an increased percentage in commission, earning team over-rides, or simply the satisfaction of introducing someone to the business, you will experience an amazing high.

Once that buzz has levelled out you will probably think, 'Oh my goodness, what do I do now?' This is quite usual - especially if you have never held a management role or been a leader of people before.

Fear Not! The best way to lead is by example, so read on.

The first thing to remember - and this should give you some confidence - is that your new recruit knows less about the business than you. However little experience you have, they will have less experience in this new business venture. They will look forward to hearing from you on how to kick-start their business and how to best work at it.

In this chapter, I will discuss several key points that you need to be aware of. I will also share ideas/activities that you can implement like empowering team members, and buddying up people. Additionally, I will touch on the difficult subject of conflict within a team.

If you just remember these two things —'Do as I do, not as I say', and 'Lead by Example' you won't go too far wrong as a leader.

Key Point 1

Do As I Do, Not As I Say!!!

Whatever you want your team to do, whatever they need to do to enjoy success, you need to have done it, or be willing to do it yourself. I have never asked a team member to do something I wouldn't do myself; it just wouldn't be fair or right. If there are activities that you no longer do (perhaps because you don't enjoy them and your business is at the stage where they are no longer essential) remember that your team member needs to incorporate this activity as their business is still in the early stages. Therefore, you need to start bringing these activities back into your business too. As an example, you may no longer participate in 'Table Top' events because you are skilled at generating leads from presentations. You may think that because you have past experience you can refer to that when teaching new team members. Due to the ever-changing environment, you need to experience what it feels like to do a Table Top event currently as opposed to historically. Social/Direct selling is a dynamic business and you need to be aware of any changes that have occurred. As a team leader you will have to come out of your 'comfort zone' frequently and do things that you would prefer to have left behind!

Key Point 2

Lead by Example

Implement the following habits, if you haven't already done so:

a. Set yourself short/medium/long term goals and **share these** with your team.

b. Present a **regular** number of sales presentations each week/service a **regular** number of customers – consistency is the key.

c. Ensure you **always** coach your hosts if you are a party planner so that your presentations are successful.

d. Consistently generate leads.

e. Consistently recruit.

f. Plan your work schedule so that **you control** the hours you work.

g. Plan team meetings and ensure that they are **FUN** - always have a training session during these meetings.

h. Analyse your own business to identify areas of strength and areas to develop.

i. Work with your up-line **as well as** your down-line.

People sometimes ask, 'Why work with your up-line, once you are established and successful?'

The short answer is that they will have more experience than you in most cases and it demonstrates to your team that you can still gain support and help whatever your level in the business. In addition, when your own team members follow your example and continue to work with you as they build a team, you build relationships with their teams too. By building relationships with second and subsequent lines of your down-line, if one of your team leaders leaves - thus their team 'rolls up' to you - there is a higher chance of retaining the inherited team members. I have seen many cases where a team leader has left a business, and their team leave soon after, due to the fact that there is no relationship with their 'new' leader.

Interesting Fact

When the DSA did some research (in the 1990's as I recall, but don't quote me on that) most people who left a Direct Selling business did so because they had no relationship or support from their up-line leader. It wasn't because they were not earning money, or enjoying their business.....surprising isn't it?

Key Point 3

Develop your Skills

To lead a team effectively you need to hone your basic business activities such as generating leads, recruiting, host coaching, booking presentations and generating incremental sales. This should come with practise. One way to improve is to ask someone else (usually your up-line) to observe and coach you. Of course, you can self-coach too. After every business activity, simply say to yourself, 'What did I do well and what could I have done better?' To develop your team members you need to become more skilled at observing them in action, giving constructive feedback, training and coaching.

Note: I will explain the difference between training and coaching in this chapter but will cover these topics more in depth in Chapter 6.

Let me begin with feedback; all feedback has to be constructive and honest. There is no point in telling someone, 'That was great', if it wasn't. Conversely, there is no need to look for something they didn't do so well, if in fact, it was done extremely well. Of course, if they ask you, 'What can I improve on?' you need to discuss the activity with them. Ask, 'What do you feel you could do differently', or 'Which aspect of the activity do you feel you want to improve?' Only then will you be able to coach them. Someone once told me that it is better to build on someone's strengths than to point out their weaknesses! I believe a good coach, who builds on a person's strengths, will inspire that person to leave the session wanting to try out the coaching method taught. This is called self-coaching, and a good coach will sow the seed for the coachee to try this out on their own, in a safe environment.

When you give feedback, your tone of voice is extremely important, as is your body language. You need to be 'actively listening', your body language needs to be relaxed (not nervous or tense), and your tone of voice needs to be calm and neutral. Using either a slightly angry/loud, or gentle/weak, voice won't bring results. Your team member will no doubt be apprehensive about what you have to say; I have encountered very few people who enjoy being observed, so be aware of this when you feedback.

Feedback needs to be approached in this order:

1. Praise/Recognition.

2. Discuss what they did well and how they can build on this to strengthen it further.

3. Identify a maximum of three development areas.

Here is an outline of a 'feedback' conversation, after observing a group presentation, or one to one selling opportunity:

You: 'Sam, you did really well there, you obviously know your products inside out and back to front'.

Sam: 'Well, I use them all the time so feel I know what I am talking about I suppose'.

You: 'Yes, I particularly liked the way you link-sold the body cream and the shower gel when Noreen asked about how long the cologne would last. Telling her to layer the three products so that the fragrance would last longer, was an excellent tip for her. Do you do this with all of your customers?'

Sam: 'No, it was because you were there if I am honest!'

You: 'I guessed you might say that (said with a smile). However, due to your love of the products, you are a really confident seller. If you remember to link-sell to all of your customers it would be well reflected in your earnings!'

You: 'How do you feel today went? Is there anything you would do differently, or add in to your next presentation?'

Sam: 'Well I ended up with a nice sale, but I think I forgot to mention the business opportunity'.

You: 'Yes, you did! I wanted to butt in - but it was your appointment! Have you thought about having something with you that reminds you to mention this? I notice you didn't have a business opportunity brochure with you to hand. Perhaps if you ensured that you carried one with you at all times it would remind you to talk about it'.

Sam: 'Good idea - I must admit I tend to focus on the sales!'

You: 'OK. Sam, tell me how you follow up on your customers after a presentation?'

Sam: 'I tend to phone them as and when I remember or when I need sales for an incentive!'

You: 'Ok - well it's good that you recognise that. However, have you thought of it from the customer's point of view? They might prefer to know that you will follow up. Imagine if you purchased a consumable product, ran out and then couldn't find where to re-purchase? Would it be more helpful, and inspire confidence, if the salesperson said, 'Sam, thanks for your order, I will call you in a couple of months to see if you need to re-order or if I can help you with anything else'

Sam: 'I never thought of it that way before and didn't want to come across as pushy. Thanks for your input!'

Note: Of course, interspersed in this conversation would be tips and advice… but you get the gist?

You then need to write down the action points from this feedback session so that when you next speak to Sam you can follow up and ensure that your observation and feedback are being implemented.

Tip: I remember going to a presentation where I literally had to sit on my hands and keep my mouth buttoned. The consultant that I was there to observe had clearly not checked out the seating or her audience. Consequently, she was not only talking to just three of the guests (as the others couldn't even see her) but she had no idea which products would interest them either. She could not have made even one host coaching call! She didn't mention the job opportunity, her kit wasn't in pristine condition and she had forgotten her host's name!

When feeding back, I picked up on the three most important points and left the rest for another time because I didn't want to completely demoralise her!

Training versus Coaching

Training is needed when someone has either not performed an activity before, or when they want to increase their skill level.

Coaching is beneficial when somebody has the information and experience to implement a task, but they want to become more skilled to increase results.

New team members need training on different aspects of the business such as:

1. Generating leads.

2. Following up on all activities. *

3. Booking presentations/one to one appointments.

4. Gaining product knowledge.

5. Managing administration.

6. Selling product.

7. Selling the business opportunity.

8. Host coaching.

9. Planning business activities.

10. Time management.

11. How the career plan works.

* Follow up is needed in all activities whether after a presentation to thank the host or to call guests who couldn't attend but may want to order, book or know about the business opportunity etc.

As your team starts to become familiar with the activities listed above, coaching needs to be introduced, especially if they want to build and develop a team of their own.

As mentioned before, coaching is when the person being coached has experience of an activity already. A good coach asks questions of the person being coached in order to bring this knowledge out, and to find ways of improving performance.

Note: We will cover these activities in more detail in the next chapter.

Key Point 4

Buddying Up Team Members

It may surprise you to know that approximately 80% of the population are not terribly self-motivated. That's a large percentage isn't it?

In a Social/Direct selling environment you often find the most successful people are self-motivated – these are the other 20% of the population. How then, do we ensure that more than 20% of our team become motivated?

One way to do this is to 'Buddy Up' team members so that they work together and motivate each other. When buddying up, look for similarities in personalities but different business strengths.

Let's take Carly and Yvette. Both are bubbly and would be described as 'people persons'. Carly is super at recruiting and Yvette achieves fantastic sales. Carly is happy to take praise and knows she does a great job but Yvette is uncomfortable with praise and doubts herself - she is outwardly confident but inwardly insecure.

How does buddying up help both of these?

Let's imagine they have twice weekly, fifteen-minute, phone calls - where the sole focus is on each of their businesses.

By discussing their successes - each sharing what they did and how they did it – then voicing which aspect of business each of them would be working on in the coming week, both should see an improvement. In addition, they need to hold each other accountable by agreeing to share what they have done differently and how this has impacted results on the next call. Discussing business activities with a peer adds a new way of looking at things and can impact results as long people are willing to change and do things differently. Carly will enjoy the praise that Yvette will surely give. When Carly reciprocates (as she surely will), Yvette will start to realise that she IS successful at selling and this will improve her insecurity issues over time. It is what we call a 'win-win' situation.

Another benefit is that neither of them can say, 'It's OK for you', because they are peers as opposed to team leader and team member, although both are successful in different aspects of the business.

When buddying people up you need some ground rules. I suggest:

a. Each pre-arranged phone call (focus call) is for a maximum twenty minutes. This keeps the focus on business.

b. If one of the parties is feeling a little low, the job of the buddy is to let them explain why they feel like this and then to 'bring them back to the positive', NOT to moan with them!

c. After listening to any challenges from their buddy, the buddy partner takes a deep breath, smiles, and says, 'OK I empathise with you, now that you have got that off your chest let's discuss how we can ensure that next week is more successful for both of us'.

Key point 5

Empowering Team Members

Possibly the most important reason as to why we need to empower others is to impart confidence and skills to enable them to build their own team. This benefits them and you.

I believe that in most business (and life) situations, two people work best together when there is something in it for both of them. When someone works on something purely for self-gain it can be seen as greedy and selfish and can be divisive. If a team leader wants to recognised, as 'best in the team' (I have known some who almost want to be worshipped) they don't create empowered, successful, independent people and this goes against the grain in the world of Social/Direct selling. Rather like a parent who 'does it all', then wonders why their offspring are still dependant as adults, if you encourage independence in your team you will find yourself with team members who fly!

I have compiled a list to help you to empower your team:

a. From the very beginning of their career ask your team members to help out at meetings. Whether this is making the coffee, writing and distributing name badges or setting out the room doesn't matter - they will start to feel included and useful. Always recognise the helpers during the meeting too!

b. Find out what people are skilled at doing, then ask them to present/train on this at a team meeting/training session.

c. Observe them doing an activity such as generating leads/running an event and ask them to speak on a team conference call.

d. For those who aspire to become a team leader, or those you know would make a good team leader, ask them to present a section of 'New Team Member Training' at your next session.

e. When team members ask you to do something for them, for example follow up a lead/train a new recruit offer to observe them doing this activity instead. Don't do it for them. If they are really nervous, offer to do the activity WITH them.

f. Offer plenty of support and recognition. Feedback constructively.

g. Ensure they have the knowledge needed before you ask them to undertake a task.

h. Never criticise or reprimand in front of others. Any negative feedback needs to be given individually and with tact.

Key Point 6

A Structure for Meetings

The simplest thing to do here is to announce at the beginning of the meeting that there are some housekeeping points that you need to share. Include:

a. Fire drill instructions.

b. Where the bathrooms are located.

c. Asking delegates to turn mobile phones off whilst in the meeting.

d. An explanation the format of the meeting – include times of comfort breaks.

e. A brief run through of the Agenda –including timings of each session, how any informal break-out sessions will function, and re-iterate what time you are planning to finish.

Finally, make your audience aware of 'meeting etiquette' by saying, 'If you have any little moans or groans please see me at the end of the meeting, as it is important we cover the Agenda. If you are worried that you may forget something that comes to mind during the meeting just pop it on a post-it note and I will collect these in later. I call this 'Parking Your Concern'.

During the meeting if anyone does voice a negative comment just remind them to 'park their concern' and tell them you will address it with them after the meeting. If you say this with a smile, it works best and diffuses a potentially awkward situation.

When presenting yourself at team meetings you need to be professional but also fun! People join Social/Direct selling companies for something a little different...most traditional business meetings are rather serious, and full of people saying what they think they ought to say, in order to 'toe the company line'. This is not what you want in your meeting; you want to encourage free and open discussion.

Although you will be the main presenter at team meetings, ensure that you are not the only one! A variety of speakers for tone of voice, speed of speech and delivery of information is important for the audience. Involve those team members who want to grow their businesses, treat them like Leaders from the start. Involve those who are successfully working their business.

A flip chart is essential at team meetings, even if you present by way of power-points or a slide presentation. Flip charts aid presenters and the audience. Presenters can easily jot down any salient points that come to mind as they are presenting. This allows the audience the luxury of taking notes fairly easily even if they cannot quite keep up with the spoken word.

Note: However small your team, do not be tempted to sit down when speaking at a team meeting. Stand up even if you remain by your seat. You will look and feel more professional. People are more likely to listen to you as opposed to chatting to the person next to them. It is good for those in your team to see you behaving like a leader. When they decide the time is good for them to build a team they will have had a good example to follow!

Tip: A very successful man, and head of several Social/Direct selling companies, once told me that 90 is a key number. People make up their minds about you in 90 seconds. I always bear this point in mind when I am taking a meeting.

90 minutes is the maximum time that anyone can hold an audience for.

Therefore, ensure that any meeting sessions finish on or before 90 minutes. Even if you go back to the topic after, take a break when 90 minutes have elapsed!

Conflict within a Team

This is a difficult situation in any business and conflict is likely to happen at some point. Why? Because we are human beings – warts and all! When two people have opposing points of view and want to air them (often in front of others) you need to take the role of arbitrator. You cannot be seen to favour one over the other. Even when you can see the validity of both parties' views, you still have to be diplomatic in what you say and how you say it. It is impossible for everyone to agree with each other all of the time. As a leader, you need to ensure that conflict doesn't get out of hand and have an adverse effect on the team. When you find yourself in this situation you will need to speak with each party individually. Inform them that they need to 'agree to disagree' for the sake of the team. Team dynamics can be challenging but they are also rewarding when handled well. You have to remain impartial at all times.

Dealing with 'Awkward and Disruptive' Personalities

Being totally honest here and not 'wrapping it up in cotton wool', we have to acknowledge that some people in this world are just negative and nearly always 'see the bad' in others. The only way to deal with a negative/argumentative/awkward/disruptive team member is through a one-to-one meeting and face to face is best as over the phone or via written communication things can be misconstrued.

It is never easy, and you may feel awkward, but there is no other way to do this.

Tactfully explain to them that not everyone shares the same opinion or working method (after all, a team of clones would be rather boring) but that we all have to listen to others and we can agree to disagree without upsetting each other. Many people in our industry end up making very good friends within a team. However, the most important relationships within a team are 'Good Working Relationships'.

The best thing about this profession is that people are self-employed and can choose who they spend most of their work-time with. If two people don't get along then surely they can just tolerate and be polite to each other for the sake of the whole team. As a team leader you can never be seen to take sides. You have to remain impartial - that's a rule you set for yourself!

You may find one or two team members consistently receive the most recognition from you due to the fact that they are the most focused on their business, which makes them more successful. This can cause 'discontent' amongst their peers; people are complex and emotional beings and jealousy can exist within any team. One way to help (after all you cannot simply stop recognising these people when they have earned the recognition) is to find other things besides hard results to recognise. You could add in any of these categories: 'Most Loyal Team Member', 'Most Reliable Team Member' (always helps out in a crisis), and 'Beat Your Best', (when someone beats their own results from last month). This ensures that those who add value to the team, (but will never be the highest flyer), enjoy visibility and status amongst their peers.

Chapter 5

Time Management for Leaders

In the previous book in this series I touched on 'How to manage your Time'. As a leader, is it even more important that you plan and use your time effectively! After all, you only have a finite number of hours to work and once you have a team of your own there are many more activities that you need to undertake. The way forward is therefore to work smart instead of hard. Let's look at a couple of instances where you can work smart.

1. Customer care calls are a great asset to your business (as mentioned in a previous chapter) and you can set up three-way calling very easily. This way, team members can listen in to your calls from their homes. The call can be used as a training session - although it is only polite to let the customer know that you have a new team member listening in for training purposes. In my experience, I have found that the customer is more likely to be receptive to what you have to offer, and curious about what your 'job' is when they know a 'trainee' is on the line! On reading this you ought to be having a 'light-bulb moment' here...someone curious about your job equals a prospective recruit! An added benefit to you and your team member is that this 'on the job training' saves time and money (no travelling costs).

2. Imagine that you have a team member who wants to improve their demonstrating skills, in order to increase the sales they achieve at a presentation. What could be better than letting them observe you? Post presentation they can feedback/ask questions, and you can coach/train them immediately whilst things are still fresh in their mind. This is much smarter than having to find an additional time slot in order to train/coach that team member on product presentation.

Activity: In our profession most of the training required by team members can be done on the job. Take five minutes now to jot down some of your day-to day business activities (such as host coaching and following up prospective recruits) and tick all of those that could be used as 'on the job training sessions' for team members.

Five Top Tips for excellent Time Management

1. Always try to have a team member who wants/needs to improve their phone skills, listening in as you make lead follow-up/host coaching calls.

2. Never have an empty passenger sea,t if you are on your way to a product presentation/coffee meeting. Take a prospective recruit or team member with you.

3. When you present team meetings, have potential team leaders help you to plan, prepare, and present.

4. Use a Telephone Conference Calling facility to train several team members on one topic. Try not to make one to one training calls. A training call of thirty minutes, multiplied by three people, means an hour and a half of you time versus thirty minutes for the same three people who are on just one call! In addition, the three people can learn from each other.

5. After every work session ask yourself if you 'worked smart' or 'worked hard'!

Leadership Duties

Here, I have listed a brief table of some of the activities that you will undertake as a team leader.

Note: Ensure that anything listed under the third column titled, 'Management Activities', does not take up more than twenty percent of your working hours.

Leadership Activities	Communication Activities	Management Activities
Follow-Up Phone Calls	Team Meeting	Newsletter
Lead Generation Phone Calls	One – to – Ones	Planning Team Meetings
Personal Recruiting	Coaching Calls/Meetings	Planning Incentives
Host Coaching	Focus Groups	Meeting with other Team Leaders
Personal Presentations	Team Training	Planning New Season Launches
Team Events (fetes etc.)	Conference Calls	General Administration

Every 'Leadership' and 'Communication' activity listed on the above grid is an opportunity for you to be observed. Whether this is a team member observing and helping you at a training event, or a potential recruit accompanying you to a presentation, this is excellent use of doubling up. You are doing you own work and training other people at the same time, which is working SMART, not working hard!

Split Page Diary

Do you find your diary or To Do list seems endless? Does this cause you stress? Be honest! To ensure that you don't have too many stressful situations a 'Split Page Diary' may help. This is a simple system where you split your day into two sections. One section contains a list of activities that are critical to the business. These are '**Must Do**' activities. The other section contains a list of activities that would be,

'Nice to Do' which will grow your business but are not priorities for that day.

An example of a split page Diary:

Wednesday 17 February 2015

Must do !!	Nice to do
1 Host coaching call - Jo Banks/Lee Smith	1 Shop for recognition gifts for March
2 Book interview - Dan Brown	2 Call Sam to see if she needs any more tips for increasing sales
3 Compile X amount of Host Packs	3 Sift through Linked-In to see if any updates are relevant for me
4 'Bookings Training' Conference Call 10.00 am	4 Pop in on new recruit Mo to see if he wants some 'loan product' to try out
5 Plan Team Meeting for Friday	5
6 Mid-month recognition email	6
7	7

As you will determine from this example, if you don't get the **Nice-to-Do** jobs done that's OK. You just roll them forward, but the **Must-Do** tasks are not optional.

Chapter 6

Training and Coaching

Coaching → Training → Observing (cycle)

The above diagram depicts how training and coaching are part of an endless cycle of helping others to reach peak performance. You will see that observing is part of the cycle – I cannot stress just how important observing someone at work is! People may tell you what they feel they do well, or not. You may **think** you know what they do well, or not. But it is only when you take the time to observe and then feedback constructively, that you will find you truly develop others.

In Chapter 4 we touched on the difference between training and coaching and the need for both activities. We will now look at these in more detail.

Training

People learn with both sides of the brain. Some people naturally use the left side more, whilst others favour the right side. It is thought that those with a tendency to use the left side are more logical, and those using the right side more are creative, but I don't claim to be a psychologist so can't prove this theory. What it does tell me is that we need to ensure that we switch on both sides of the brain when training and coaching someone – we can do this by appealing to all five senses, which are:

1. Sight
2. Smell
3. Taste
4. Touch
5. Hearing

In addition to this, when you are about to embark on a training programme for somebody on a one-to-one basis, it is worthwhile asking them how they prefer to learn; is it by reading information, through listening, by watching, or do they learn by physically performing tasks? If someone prefers to read, arm them with all the materials they need, then break this down into manageable chunks and discuss what they have learnt after each study period. If they prefer to watch, take them along to various activities of yours and spend time afterwards discussing what they have learnt. Naturally, you will include other methods of training but if someone really has to 'do it for themselves' there is little point in just sending them away with reading material, having been 'talked at' during a training session. Of course, it is not such a simple matter when training a group of people where you need to ensure that you cover as many methods as possible. It helps if you can appeal to the senses listed above. Sight and Hearing are fairly easy to cover and I will touch on these at the end of this chapter.

So, let's take a more in-depth look at Training, Observing and Coaching, and how these activities will develop your team.

When someone new joins a business, or starts a new job, they need direction. Hence, in some Social/Direct selling businesses team leaders are awarded the title of Director. As a team leader it is part of your job to give direction to your team. When you have a new team member you need to teach them what to do and how to do it, which also means setting expectations based on what they have told you they want from their business. After all, without any expectation being set, how can someone know if they are successful? Additionally, how will you know when to praise and recognise your team members if you don't know what they were aiming for?

Other words for **Expectations** are **Goals or Targets.** Not many people feel comfortable setting goals (as I have found out from experience). Even fewer people want to work to targets.

I believe it is all about the words themselves; 'goal' and 'target' are a little off putting after all. When working with people who say they dislike setting goals, I ask, 'When you set out on a journey do you have a time and destination in mind?' 'Of course', they invariably reply. I then explain that this is, in effect, 'a goal'. If they hadn't set that goal they would still be driving around goodness knows where. I explain that we all set goals every single day of our lives - it is just that we don't use the word 'goal'. However, you must remember that goal setting needs to be kept fairly basic, and the goal needs to be the goal of the person you are working with- **it is not your goal**!

Goals can only be reached by doing some sort of activity. Thus when training or coaching you need to bear this in mind – there is no point setting goals unless they can be achieved so the activity level needed should be physically possible for the person whose goal it is.

As soon as any team member joins your team you need to devise an action plan with them, which means setting a goal (or expectation) and then listing the action (activities) that need to be undertaken in order to achieve the goal.

It is a good idea to use a simple 'Business Plan' form which you could develop yourself if the company you are part of doesn't already have a template. You could use the Potential Business Plan contained in Chapter 1, just take 'potential' out of it! You need to consider:

1. How much your team member wants to earn (GOAL).

2. How many sales presentation they need to undertake each week to meet their required earnings (ACTIVITY).

OR:

2a. Total number of customers needed to be seen, to ensure enough product is purchased each week, to meet their required earnings (ACTIVITY).

Can you see how the simple goal of wanting to earn £XX can then be broken down into just two activities which will help ensure the goal is met?

Looking at this simple statistic you now need to set some action points.

An example would be:

Neil has said he would like do one group presentation each week and wants to earn £400 per month.

He has plenty of names on his contact list and a potential 12 hosts for 'practise presentations'.

He also has more time slots available should he need to work them.

You know that an average presentation in your area is around £300 and he will earn 20% commission to begin with, giving him £60 earnings per party.

One party a week gives him £240.00 earnings per month on average, leaving him £160 short of his goal.

You now need to discuss with Neil the possibility of adding in another 2 - 4 presentations each month which will help him to achieve his earnings goal. If he is in agreement you now need to set some expectations, which will include:

1. Developing his contact list to give him more opportunities to look for bookings.

2. Increasing the number of phone calls he makes each week to offer presentations.

3. Increasing his bookings to two a week which will give room for postponements.

His monthly plan may look like this:

Week One:

Presentation for Jo Brookes

Presentation (postponed)

Week Two:

Presentation for Sam Smith

Presentation for Alex Brown

Week Three:

Presentation for Max Jones

Presentation for Pat Black

Week Four:

Presentation for Lee Green

Presentation (postponed)

Holding six firm presentations will earn him £360; not quite his goal of £400 but don't forget it is early days and his average will go up as he gains experience in selling product. If he can sell on a one to one basis too, then a couple of appointments could take him just above his goal. If he really cannot fit this number of presentations in to his diary then you need to explain that his expectation is too high initially. Would he be happy with £240 of earnings - after all this is still extra money in his pocket? If not, what would he be happy with? Through discussion and through doing the math you should be able to come to a satisfactory result for Neil.

Also check whether there are other cash/product/travel incentives offered by the company that he would like to earn, as these are good goal setting tools too. Remember -

cash is not the only benefit to a Social/Direct se business. Finally, discuss how to showcase and sell product so that Neil could potentially increase his earnings via the Internet, by attending fetes and fayres and by using telesales.

Whenever a member of your team first tries a new activity, whether it's presenting product for the first time, manning a stand at a fete, host coaching, or making customer care calls, you need to ensure that you have taught them **'how to do it'**. We often tell people **what** to do but it is the **'how to'** that is most important.

After all - Imagine telling a child to tie their shoe laces without ever showing them 'how to', or telling a puppy to 'sit' without gently pressing on its back end!

Observing

You need to observe team members as they perform different activities, for the following reasons:

1. To recognise and praise.

2. To help them develop strengths.

3. To identify and build on any weaker areas.

Observing will also help you, as you are bound to pick up on things they do well that you perhaps could use in your own activities and in training others. You can also invite them to present on a topic which is one of their strong points, at a team meeting. This gives them recognition and kudos and ensures your team meetings are varied in speakers and ideas. After all a team meeting is just that - a meeting and sharing of ideas and tips for the team. It is not your meeting and you shouldn't be the only speaker.

...unless you have a fantastic memory, do ...ke a few notes. Then your feedback ...used and constructive, which is more ... both parties.

...ning

First of all here are a few important points for you to keep in mind as you begin coaching:

1. A coach listens.

2. The job of a coach is to bring out the best in someone.

3. You never stop coaching.

4. You never stop needing coaching, whether you self-coach or you use a coach.

5. It is rare that anyone is so **expert** in any activity/subject that they don't need any more coaching. Look at top athletes; they are coached until the day they retire!

Fun Note: An ex is something in the past.

A spurt is a drip of water.

Who wants to be called an expert?

Many years ago I attended a training course which focused on **Coaching for Enhanced Performance;** several key points made an impression on me:

1. You don't need to be a champion athlete yourself, in order to **coach a champion** athlete!

2. It is difficult to Coach someone to perform an activity without showing them **'how'**.

3. A good coach **encourages** the coachee to come up with the answers.

4. Coaching encourages creativity and **'out of the box thinking'**.

5. Coaches cannot 'tell', but can make suggestions with the **permission** of the coachee.

6. Coaching **increases** performance.

One of the exercises we were asked to perform to encourage out of the box thinking was pretty simple. You could try this with your team.

Group Exercise

Stage 1

Everyone stands in a circle and the coach holds a large ball. The coach then instructs the group that:

'The object of this exercise is that every person gets to take control/hold/have contact with the ball!'

Note: When instructing the group at the beginning of the exercise, be sure to use the phrase above. You will see why when you get to the end of the exercise. Don't labour the point, and speak fairly quickly as you don't want too much explanation!

The coach starts off the activity by, 'Showing How', thus throws the ball randomly to a member of the team who then follows the lead and throws the ball randomly to another member of the team.

Others follow until the coach shouts, 'Stop'.

Stage 2

Coach explains that they want to speed the exercise up.

Coach shouts out a name and throws the ball to named person.

Note: If the team are starting to 'get it' they may throw the ball to someone closer to them- that's OK!

Again, others follow until the coach shouts, 'Stop'

Stage 3

Coach explains to the group that they need to speed up yet again and chooses a leader to take the place of the coach.

Note: What happens next is that the chosen leader may suggest, 'Just pass the ball to the person immediately next to you', as this speeds the exercise up. (If you feel generous you could allow ten seconds or so for the group to discuss how to move the ball more quickly).

Stage 4

What the group should come up with is that the quickest way for every group member to have contact with the ball is for one person to hold it high, whilst the rest of the group to run to that person and put their finger on the ball.

It may be that the group figure this out for themselves or it may be that you have to explain this!

This is a quick, fun, interactive group exercise to get the brain working creatively but do take note that it works best in large groups.

Any exercise that get your team thinking about how to improve performance by simply doing an activity in a slightly different way can be classed as performance coaching!

One of the most important skills for a coach to develop is that of - **Active Listening.**

As I may have already said, coaching is about listening actively and asking effective, thoughtful questions. Here are a few open ended questions that I have found to be effective:

How do you feel about your business right now?

What do you feel are your strengths?

Which areas of your business would you like to improve?

What do you enjoy doing?

What do you not enjoy?

Tell me how you (insert activity here)? Does this bring the results you want?

By asking these you will get a good idea of how your coachee is feeling about their business, what they feel they need help with, and what they enjoy doing. You can start to form your coaching plan, and feedback to build on strengths, before discussing how to improve any weaknesses. This is positive coaching and builds a good coach/coachee relationship.

Setting Goals via Coaching and Training

During your career you will no doubt coach and train, and be coached and trained, many times. Through these activities you will set goals. One thing that is critical is that you ensure all goals encompass the word SMART. A SMART goal is:

Specific

Measurable

Action Orientated

Realistic

Timed

This is nothing new, and most of you will have encountered SMART goals before. There are some variations on the definition of a SMART goal however, so I will briefly, and simply, cover what I deem to be a SMART goal.

Specific – the goal has to be clearly defined or identified – not vague as in 'I would like to increase my sales'. How do you want to increase your sales? By selling more products at presentations, or online or….?

Measurable – how will you measure the goal, how will you know if progress is being made – can you put in 'mile markers' to measure progress to ensure you reach your goal?

Action- Orientated – this is the activity that needs to happen in order to achieve the goal.

Realistic – is the goal realistic? For example, if I were to say I wanted to lose a stone - and only had a couple of weeks in which to do it - that would be totally unrealistic for me. However, 1-2lb a week over ten weeks would be realistic, based on my knowledge of myself and my weight.

Timed – all goals need a time in which to achieve them, going back to my goal of losing weight I could put a time limit of seven weeks to lose a stone (at 2lb a week as above).

Here is an example of a SMART goal:

I want to lose a stone in weight – this is specific.

I will aim to lose between 1 - 2lb a week – this is measurable.

I need to reduce my calorific intake and to exercise at least three times a week for twenty minutes at a time – this is action orientated.

This weight loss is in line with NHS guidelines and I have done is before – it is realistic.

Losing 1 – 2lb a week I am setting my goal of losing a stone over ten weeks – the goal is timed.

Now, I suggest you take thirty minutes to sit down, reflect and set yourself a SMART goal using the above criteria. It can only result in moving your business forward after all!

As promised near the start of this chapter, here are a few ideas to ensure you engage the senses of sight and hearing when training team members.

Sight – Use posters and positive signage like motivational quotes placed around the room and on surfaces such as spare tables, window ledges, shelves and cupboards. You could use some short clips from DVD's for delegates to watch. Try to include short sessions on laptops or tablets where delegates can look up information and then share what they have found to be interesting. Remember I mentioned a visual aid designed for use during presentations, which consisted of sheets of paper that would concertina out? You could use this idea for training meetings too.

Hearing –Your audience need to be kept entertained. How about using a CD or Radio clip? For example when teaching how to enhance listening skills you could play an extract from a Radio show and then ask questions to see how well the audience listened. During verbal presentations in particular, a change of speaker is important. Even when you are the main presenter could you bring in some interactive sessions? Maybe after twenty minutes of you talking you could invite questions before you move on to the next point you want to make? It is important to change your tone of your voice, and even the speed of your voice can be varied.

Note: As mentioned in the previous chapter, people can only take in information for ninety minutes – all training (and coaching) activities need to have a break at ninety minute intervals.

Chapter 7

Coming Out of Your Comfort Zone.....often!

Why do you think it is important to come out of your 'Comfort Zone'?

The simple answer is 'development' – not only for your business, but for you personally!

However, there is more to moving outside of your comfort zone than you may think. When you constantly work within your comfort zone, you will never know the feeling of absolute elation, having accomplished something new. You will not be stretching yourself and will not be achieving the results that you are capable of. I believe if you come out of your comfort zone regularly you will enjoy more success in your business; you will develop useful business skills and learn what works and what doesn't!

Now, you may be thinking that you enjoy your work as it is - you may even give yourself a pat on the back for a job well done from time to time - but the real excitement and sheer feel-good factor comes from having done something you either feared (remember, **FEAR** is **F**un, **E**asy **A**nd **R**ewarding) or felt you would not be able to accomplish.

Be **Kinder*** to yourself by coming out of your comfort zone.

Be **Kinder*** to your team by practising tough love!

When you do something that doesn't feel comfortable or familiar, you are demonstrating to team members that you are prepared to go through what they may be going through. Remember 'Do as I do, not as I say', and 'Leading by Example'! By doing this, and encouraging others to do the same, you are setting a good example for team members to follow, thus creating more successful, empowered and motivated people.

Remember - the key to a successful team is a successful leader.

Remember - the simplest way to 'follow the leader' is to make your activities duplicable.

Note: Sometimes we work within our comfort zone just because we can – after all we don't have a 'boss' or a 'manager' to report to, so we can choose which activities we implement in our business can't we? Be your **own Best Boss** by stretching and pushing yourself just a little bit more!

Sometimes we stay in our comfort zone because we are happy with our results. However, this is a dynamic industry and you can never rest on your laurels. If you are happy with your results now, imagine how you would feel if you achieved even better results!

Activity: Practise coming out of your comfort zone!

Before you try new business activities which challenge you, why not try something that you are a little nervous, or not confident, about in your personal life?

When you go abroad to a country where you do not speak or understand the language, what do you do?

a. Take a phrase book?

b. Speak English, and hope that you are understood?

c. Avoid conversation?

How about deliberately going to a market stall or small shop and trying to converse, having jotted down a couple of key words? It is amazing how, having purchased a few items with the odd word and lots of pointing and nodding, you will emerge feeling pleased with yourself.

Perhaps you could try your hand at a motor racing day experience, or a balloon flight; maybe try a gliding lesson? Anything that you have never experienced before would be good to try.

If those ideas sound a bit too scary, try approaching people that you don't know - just to make small talk. You can do this as you go about your daily business – in the supermarket, at a local club or leisure centre or even out walking – a smiley 'Hello', can go a long way.

Would you feel comfortable going into a bar or restaurant on your own? If not, give it a go. I can promise you that you will still be b-r-e-a-t-h-i-n-g when you leave. Before you go in just be sure to take a couple of deep breaths and hold your head high.

At least a couple of times a week you need to try doing something different or new. This creates a habit, and ensures that you fully understand how a team member feels when they need to do an activity that is out of their comfort zone.

When you dare to step out of your 'Business Comfort Zone' these are some of the benefits you will enjoy:

Knowledge – you will learn something from each experience.

Inspiration – your team members will be inspired to try it for themselves.

New ideas – each experience will give you new ideas on how to approach similar activities.

Development – you can use the experience to develop yourself and your team.

Experience – we learn best by doing things ourselves.

Results – by trying new activities you should find results increasing.

Make a habit out of being KINDER* to yourself.

Glossary

Booking
Creating interest in and diarising, a firm date for holding a product presentation.

Career Plan
Sometimes referred to as, the Marketing, Compensation or Payment Plan. This explains what commissions and over-rides you will be paid, what you need to achieve in order to promote yourself, and illustrates any other benefits which may be available throughout your Career.

Close in Booking
A date for a product presentation which will take place within the next 6 weeks.

Collectable Products
Product ranges where items are designed to complement each other -for example a range of clothing where particular pieces work well as a 'capsule wardrobe'.

Commission
You will be paid a percentage of the sales you generate which is usually referred to as commission.

Conference
Most companies offer one or two conferences a year where they will showcase new product to be launched

and offer training. Guest speakers are used for motivation and inspiration in most cases.

Consumable Products
For example: vitamins/cosmetics/candles/food.

Direct Recruit
Someone you have personally recruited.

Distributor
Name for an Independent Direct Seller. Companies used different words to describe their direct sellers including those of Retailer, Dealer and Consultant.

Downline
Team members who, according to the Career Plan, are one or more levels down from you – they may have been recruited either by you (direct recruit) or by one of your team members (indirect recruit).

Direct Selling Association (D.S.A)
A professional body which strives to raise the profile of the Industry, and to protect interests of DSA members and consumers.

Host
Person who invites others to attend a product presentation - usually in their own home.

Host Coaching
The process of coaching the person who is hosting a product presentation, to ensure the success of the event.

Host Reward System

The way that (in most cases) companies reward and thank hosts for inviting guests along to a product presentation.

Incentives

Rewards offered to encourage activities in order to reach desired performance goals. Incentives are often in the form of cash bonus's/products/overseas trips etc.

Incremental Sales

These are over and above expected or required Sales. For example you may be required to sell £100 of product per week to achieve the earnings you want – if you sell £120 the £20 would be incremental.

Indirect recruits

People you have not personally recruited but have been recruited by one of your down-line.

Interview

Also referred to as a coffee meeting. This is when you meet up with someone to explain how your business works, so that they can make an informed decision as to whether to join the business.

Leads

Individuals who may have an interest in either products, or the business opportunity.

Leg
Once a team member starts to build a team of their own this is referred to as a 'leg' or a 'generation'.

Level
Your personally recruited team are your 1st level. When members start to recruit their own team, this second team become your 2nd level. When 2nd level team members recruit people, they become your 3rd level. NB. Check this out with your chosen company as it may vary!

Long-dated Booking
A Product Presentation scheduled for 6 months (or more) ahead.

Mass Market
Products sold inexpensively that appeal to the 'mass market' for example Avon Cosmetics, Kleeneze.

MLM
Multi-level Marketing is a structure by which the company rewards their team leaders for sales of others no matter how many levels down from them in the plan, whereas Network Marketing usually has a limit so may reward for perhaps just four or five levels down.

Monthly Planner
A simple calendar style form to enable monthly activities to be viewed at a glance – essentially used to plan the upcoming month's activities.

Multi-Channel
Product marketed via more than one channel. An example of which is Ann Summers who sell via Retail Outlets, Party plan and the Internet.

Non-Consumable Products
Items such as: clothing, kitchenware, household appliances, jewellery.

Overrides
Sometimes called team commissions this is a percentage of sales made by your team, in return for recruiting, training and supporting them.

Party Plan Business
Where sales are generated through parties (product presentations) made to a group of people who have been invited along by the Host.

Personal or Direct Recruits
People you have personally recruited.

Prospect
Someone who has expressed an interest in finding out about the business opportunity.

Recruiting
An activity whereby a Social/Direct seller meets with or talks to a person who subsequently joins the business – sometimes called sponsoring.

Referrals
Names of people who may be interested in product or the business opportunity, gained from customers, adverts or through general conversation with others.

Social/Direct Seller
An independent, self-employed person, who is part of the distribution system of a Social/Direct selling company. Social/Direct sellers are authorised to place sales orders from customers direct to the company. Orders are gained within a 'Social Selling Environment' such as a product presentation or social media.

Sponsor/Recruiter
This is the person who introduced you to the company.

Sponsor/Recruit
When someone new joins the business they can be referred to as a Recruit or a Sponsor.

Roll Up
This occurs when a person leaves the business - any people that they have recruited 'Roll-Up' to the person who recruited the person that has left.

Single Channel
Product marketed through one channel. For example solely through the Direct Sales channel.

Starter Kit
Usually this contains paperwork such as order forms, catalogues and general product literature in addition to a small amount of product to be used for demonstration purposes. May be referred to as a Distributor Kit.

Team Leader
Independent Direct Sellers who support a team of people, usually recruited by them. Sometimes referred to as a Manager or Director.

Team Meetings
These are for self-employed Social/Direct sellers to meet up with their peers. Usually led by the most senior and experienced seller in a team, Team Meetings are vehicles for recognition and Training.

Trunk Show
Another way of describing a product presentation whereby a Social/Direct seller take a sample of their product range along to a host and their guests, in order to take orders and promote the business opportunity.

Up-line
The person directly above you in the hierarchy of the Career Plan. This could be the person who recruited you, or if they have left, it could be the person who was above them, as you would usually 'roll up' to that person, should your recruiter leave.

About Leigh Walton

Leigh Walton is an accomplished Direct Sales professional, having worked in the industry for over twenty five years. She started out as a self-employed 'Avon Lady' after chatting to an Area Manager who had 'cold called' at her home. Leigh attributes her first 'lesson in Social and Direct Sales' to this ad-hoc meeting as she soon came to understand that by listening to what Leigh was saying, asking open-ended questions and then answering Leigh's needs, this Area Manager turned a 'no, I'm not interested in Avon', to a 'Yes, I'll give it a go'.

A couple of years on, Leigh was employed as an Area Manager by Avon Cosmetics; firstly appointed to cover part of inner-city Birmingham and then the upmarket town of Solihull - 'chalk and cheese' as Leigh describes them. The difference in attitude to 'Avon' in these areas tested Leigh's 'out of the box' thinking and strengthened her creativity. She is pro-active to the hilt and has also developed the ability to react to any given situation. After promotion to a training and development role with Avon her career really took off.

She was soon employed by Virgin (Vie) Cosmetics for the start-up of Richard Branson's foray into 'Party Plan', worked with the superb book publisher, 'Dorling Kindersley', where her direct approach was welcomed by the independent sales-force. Over the next couple of years Leigh was approached, and subsequently recruited, by several companies including The Pampered Chef (UK) where she was promoted to National Sales Manager.

During 2012, Leigh started to make plans to fulfil her ambition of studying for an English degree whilst also working as a self-employed Business Coach and Trainer. In April 2013 Leigh left The Pampered Chef to travel around Europe with her husband and two terriers. During this time she has also written three books and is currently studying for an Honours Degree in English Language and Literature with the Open University.

Even whilst travelling she is alert to what is happening generally 'in Sales' and whilst working her way down Croatia, upon seeing many people stood on the side of roads with large signs stating 'Apartmento', wanted to contact the agent letting her house to say, 'Have you thought of....'.

Leigh's motto of 'Life is not a Dress Rehearsal' is what drives her! In addition, a phrase learned many years ago, 'Anywhere, Anytime, Always, Ask', is one which all Social/Direct Sellers need to keep in mind. Whether in a coffee shop, a queue in a shop, chatting to someone on the train, if you remember the '4 A's' you will be giving yourself the best opportunity to become a success in Social/Direct Sales.

What are you waiting for?

If you have enjoyed this book why not let others know?

Please go to Amazon and leave a review!

Other Books by Leigh Walton

Social/Direct Selling - Yes You Can (Book One)

Travels with Martha   (2015)

More Travels with Martha   (2015)

Katie's Diary   (2015)

Letters to Sofia   (2015)

The Balloon Flight & Other Short Stories   (2015)

Connect with Leigh Walton

Twitter

>   http://twitter.com/@leighw10

Facebook

>   https://www.facebook.com/pages/Leigh-Walton-Author-Writer/747679335282745

Web Site Coming soon!

>   www.leighwalton.com

Printed in Great Britain
by Amazon